D0999876

★ IT'S MY STATE! ★

Arizona

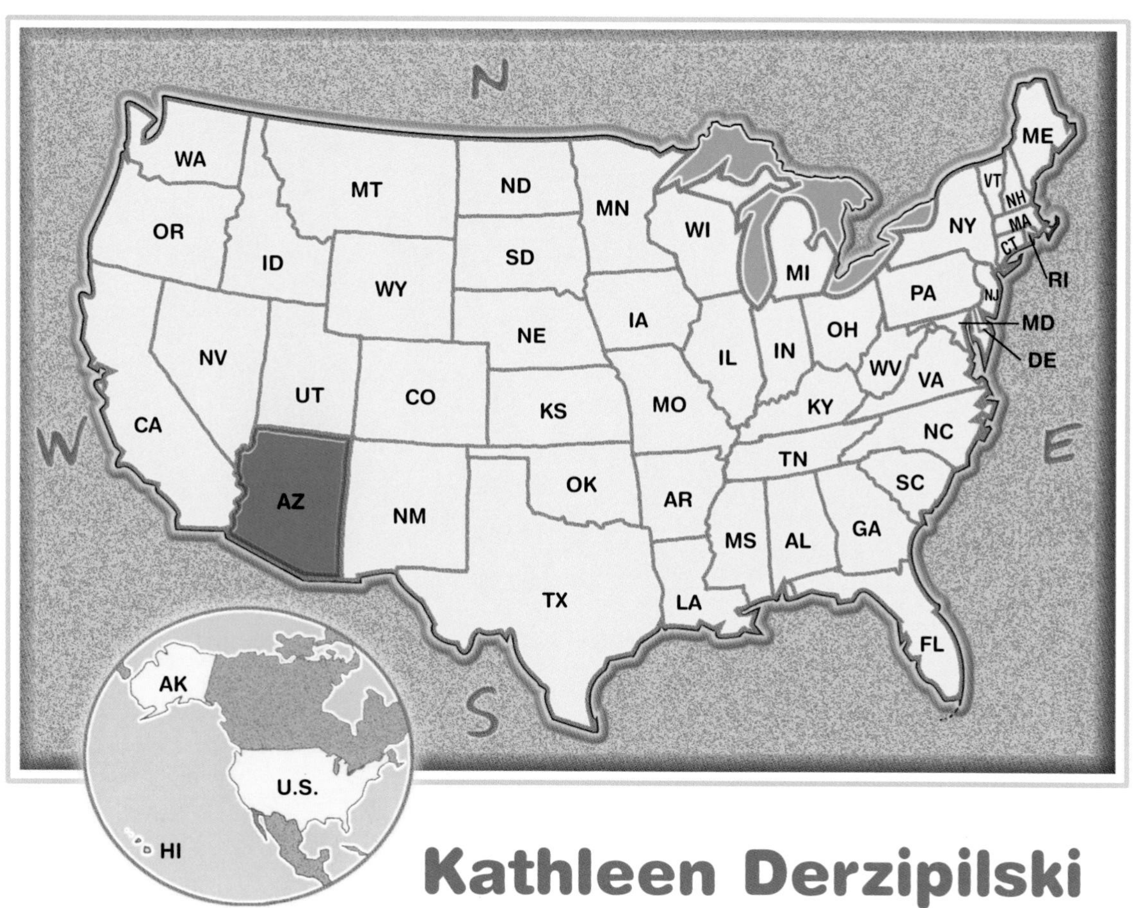

Kathleen Derzipilski

BENCHMARK BOOKS

MARSHALL CAVENDISH
NEW YORK

Series Consultant

David G. Vanderstel, Ph.D., Executive Director, National Council on Public History

With thanks to Gwen Russell Harvey, Director of Education, Arizona Historical Society, for her expert review of the manuscript.

Benchmark Books
Marshall Cavendish
99 White Plains Road
Tarrytown, New York 10591-9001
www.marshallcavendish.com

Maps and illustrations by Christopher Santoro

Library of Congress Cataloging-in-Publication Data

Derzipilski, Kathleen.
Arizona / by Kathleen Derzipilski.
p. cm. — (It's my state!)
Summary: Surveys the history, geography, government, and economy of Arizona, as well as the diverse ways of life of its people.
Includes bibliographical references and index.
ISBN 0-7614-1686-2
1. Arizona—Juvenile literature. [1. Arizona.] I. Title. II. Series.

F811.3.D47 2004
979.1—dc22
2003020349

Photo research by Candlepants, Inc.

Cover photograph: B.S.P.I. / Corbis

Back coverillustration: The license plate shows Arizona's postal abbreviation, followed by its year of statehood.

The photographs in this book are used by permission and through the courtesy of: *Corbis:* 8, 22, 31, 32, 33, 39 (top), 70 (bottom); Steve Kaufman, 4 (top); Eric and David Hosking, 4 (middle); AINCO, 5 (top); Tom Bean, 10, 64; Gerald French, 11; Greg Probst, 15, 25; Kennan Ward, 17; Alissa Crandall, 18 (middle); Buddy Mays, 18 (bottom), 27; Bettmann, 26, 51 (bottom), 59; Charles E. Rotkin, 35; Michael S. Yamashita, 36, 49; Charles O'Rear, 38; Andrew Brown / Ecoscene, 39 (low); Richard Cummins,41, 74; Mike King, 50 (middle); Catherine Karnow, 55; Joseph Sohm/ChromoSohm, Inc., 56, 61, 71 (top); Pete Saloutos, 68; Aero Graphics, Inc., 71 (bottom); Roger Ressmeyer, 72; *SuperStock:* Anthony Mercieca, 4 (bottom); Dale O'Dell, 9; Les David Manevitz, 14. *Photo Researchers, Inc.:* Richard T. Nowitz, 5 (middle); Tom McHugh, 5 (bottom), 20; Craig K. Lorenz, 13, 18 (top); David R. Frazier, 19 (top); Anthony Mercieca, 19 (bottom); Renee Lynn, 21. *Minden Pictures/Yva Momatiuk/John Eastcott: 19* (middle). *Ted Wood/Getty Images:* 40. *The Image Works:* Jack Kurtz, 43, 47, 52, 54, 66, 70 (top); David Frazier, 71 (middle). *History and Archives Division of the Arizona State Library:* 50 (top and bottom). *Cumberland County Historical Society Carlisle, PA.:* 51 (top). *Sharlot Hall Museum Photo Prescott, Arizona:* 51 (middle).*Index Stock Imagery:* Terri Froelich, 53; Gary Conner, 70 (middle). *Mark Ferri/Envision:* 67.

Series design by Anahid Hamparian

Printed in Italy

1 3 5 6 4 2

Contents

A Quick Look at Arizona 4

1 **Grand Canyon State** 7

Plants & Animals 18

2 **From the Beginning** 23

Important Dates 39

3 **The People** 41

Create a Navajo Sandpainting 44

Famous Arizonans 50

Calendar of Events 54

4 **How It Works** 57

Branches of Government 58

5 **Making a Living** 65

Recipe for Citrus Ice Cream 67

Products & Resources 70

State Flag and Seal 75

State Map 76

State Song 77

More About Arizona 78

Index 79

A Quick Look at Arizona

Nickname: Grand Canyon State

Population: 5,307,331 (2001 estimate)

Statehood: 1912

Flower: Saguaro Blossom

Saguaro blossoms grow on the tips of the arms of the saguaro cactus. The cactus first blooms when it is about fifty years old and five feet tall, and then blooms every year from mid-May to mid-June. When the blossoms bloom, large white flowers open at night and stay open through the next day. The flowers develop into sweet, juicy fruits that are full of tiny seeds.

Tree: Palo Verde

Palo verde *is Spanish for "green stick," and the tree takes its name from the green bark on its branches and trunk. Fragrant yellow flowers cover the trees in the spring. The seeds are food for beetles and a variety of rodents. The trees grow in sandy areas and rocky hillsides throughout the Sonoran Desert.*

Bird: Cactus Wren

The cactus wren is the largest wren in Arizona and the United States. Cactus wrens eat insects, spiders, and other small animals. These wrens like to build their large, round nests inside the cholla cactus. Though the outside of the cactus can be prickly, the nests inside are lined with soft feathers.

Neckwear: Bola Tie

The bola tie was invented in Arizona and many men and women living in the West wear them. The tie is made of a long leather braid and is tightened around the neck with a sliding clasp. The clasp often displays beautiful silver work with polished minerals and stones. The bola tie was adopted as the official state neckwear in 1973.

Gemstone: Turquoise

Turquoise is a blue-green gemstone that contains copper and aluminum. The gemstone has a special significance for many Native American groups of the Southwest and is used in jewelry, crafts, and ceremonies. Long ago, the native peoples of Arizona and New Mexico mined turquoise and carried the valued gem along the trade routes to Mexico.

Amphibian: Arizona Treefrog

The Arizona treefrog is one of two treefrog species native to Arizona. The small frog lives in the oak, pine, and fir forests of central Arizona's mountains. Arizona treefrogs can measure from 3/4 of an inch to 2 inches long. The pads on their toes allow the tree frogs to climb the tall trees. Their green and brown coloring camouflages the frogs.

ARIZONA

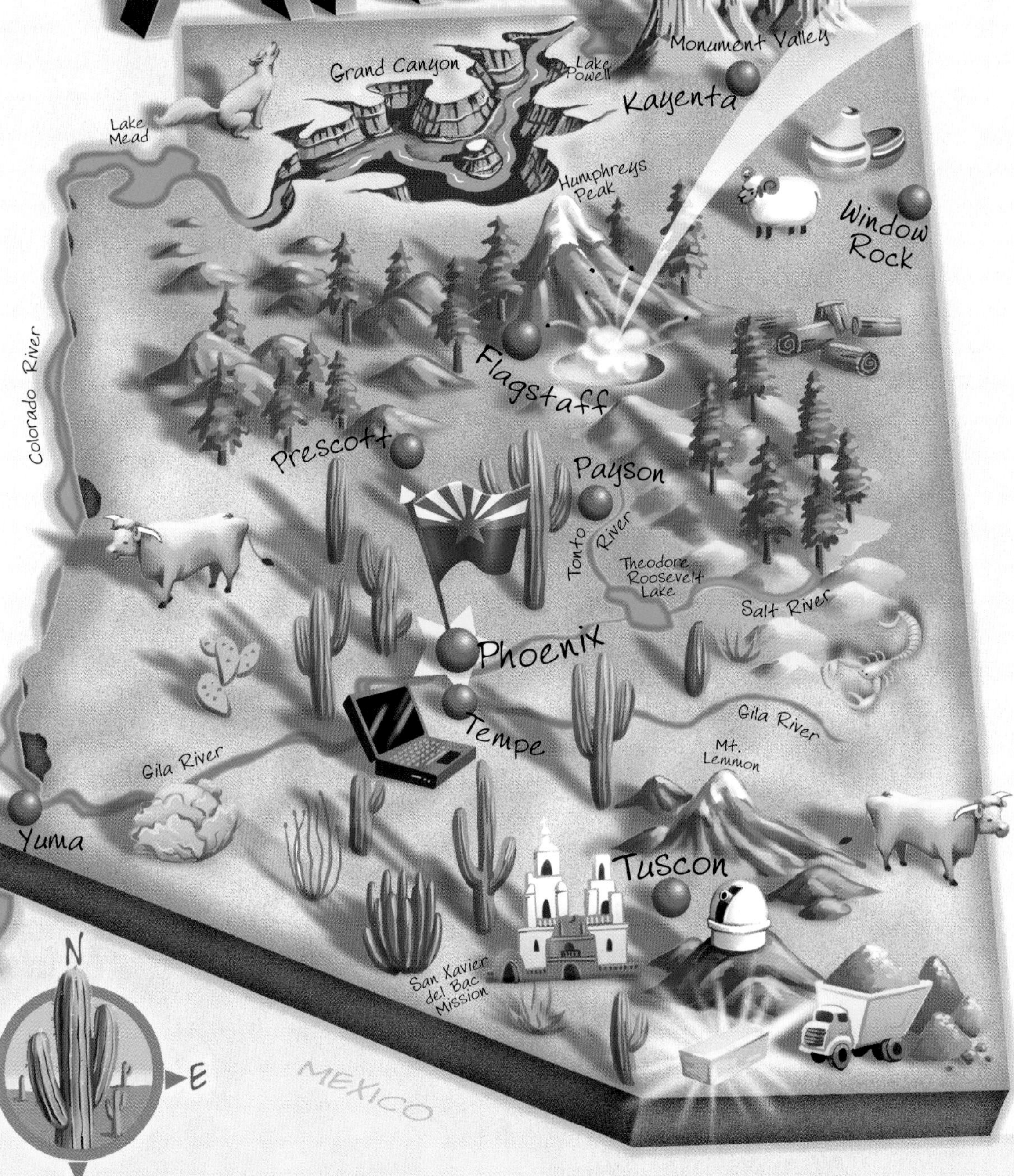

Monument Valley
Grand Canyon
Lake Powell
Kayenta
Lake Mead
Humphreys Peak
Window Rock
Colorado River
Flagstaff
Prescott
Payson
Tonto River
Theodore Roosevelt Lake
Salt River
Phoenix
Tempe
Gila River
Gila River
Mt. Lemmon
Yuma
Tuscon
San Xavier del Bac Mission
MEXICO
N
W
E
S

1 Grand Canyon State

Arizona is a large state located in the southwestern section of the United States. Of all the states it is the sixth largest. Arizona is shaped almost like a square and measures 400 miles from north to south and 310 miles from west to east. The state's total area is 113,446 square miles.

Arizona's landscape can be divided into three regions. The northern part of the state is part of the high Colorado Plateau. The southern part is the low Basin and Range region. Between these two regions is an area of mountains called the Mexican Highland division. The Mexican Highland division runs diagonally west to east across the middle of the state. The state's higher elevations—ranging from 5,000 to 8,000 feet—are in the north. The southern part of the state has lower elevations, which range from 500 to 5,000 feet.

Arizona's Borders

North: Utah
South: Mexico
East: Colorado and New Mexico
West: Nevada and California

The Colorado Plateau

The Colorado Plateau is a landscape of plateaus, mesas, and buttes covered by ancient lava flows and cut by canyons. The canyons and buttes reveal layers of stone, minerals, ash, and fossils. Many canyons were created by rivers that wore down the rocks over millions of years. The Colorado River formed the Grand Canyon—one of the most famous natural sites in the United States. Located in the western part of the Colorado Plateau, this canyon is about one mile deep, with the Colorado River flowing at the bottom. Different portions of the canyon range in width from 1 to 18 miles. The Grand Canyon is 277 miles long and splinters into many side canyons. John Wesley Powell explored the Grand Canyon and the Colorado River in 1869. He wrote about the immensity and grandeur of the canyon and described it as "a broad, deep, flaring gorge of many colors." Throughout the year, many people travel to Arizona to visit Grand Canyon National Park.

A view of the Colorado River in Grand Canyon National Park.

Visitors to Arizona can explore part of an extinct volcano at Sunset Crater Volcano National Monument.

North of the Grand Canyon is an area called the Kaibab Plateau. It is covered with a forest of ponderosa pines. South of Grand Canyon and surrounding the city of Flagstaff is the San Francisco Plateau. Hundreds of extinct volcanoes—volcanoes that are not currently erupting and will not erupt anytime in the future—can be found there. One of the volcanoes is called the San Francisco Peaks. It is a large volcanic cone with several peaks on its rim. The highest of these peaks is Humphreys Peak. It rises 12,633 feet and is the highest point in Arizona. The state's youngest volcano, Sunset Crater, erupted in 1065 C.E. For fifty years, it spewed ash, cinders, and lava.

Unique rock formations are just a few of the features that attract visitors to Arizona's Painted Desert.

Erosion—the wearing away of land by wind, water, and time—has shaped the eastern part of the Colorado Plateau. The strange shapes and rock formations of the badlands and the Painted Desert were carved by erosion. The wearing away of the land has also uncovered the mineral-filled logs of the Petrified Forest. In this forest, the wood petrified, or slowly changed into rocklike mineral-rich material. The isolated buttes and mesas of Monument Valley in northeastern Arizona were also formed by erosion. The steep slopes of the Mogollon Rim mark the southern boundary of the Colorado Plateau.

Arizona is one of the states in the Four Corners. This is the only place in the United States where the boundaries of four states meet. The other Four Corner states are Utah, Colorado, and New Mexico.

Mexican Highland

About thirty short mountain chains fill the Mexican Highland, located across the middle of the state. Movements deep inside the earth sixty million years ago formed these mountains. The mountains are rich with copper, silver, molybdenum, and other minerals. The highest mountains are forested with Douglas fir and ponderosa pine trees. Pinyon pine and juniper grow at the lower elevations.

One of Arizona's large cities, Phoenix, is located in the central part of the state. Many people come to central Arizona to visit this city. But people also come to fish in the shady streams of the Mexican Highland. In winter, many come to ski. The forests of the White Mountains in eastern Arizona are harvested for timber.

Set amid the Mexican Highland, Phoenix is a well-developed capital city with a large population and a bustling economy.

The state's second-highest mountain, Baldy Peak, is in the White Mountains. This peak rises to 11,590 feet.

Basin and Range

The Basin and Range region extends over southern Arizona. It is an expansive flat land with basins that are interrupted by abrupt, jagged mountains. The basins are shallow valleys like big, dry ponds. Erosion's effects mark this region too. The wind continues to carry away the soil and the fine sand from the dry, hard ground. The city of Tucson is located in the southern third of Arizona.

> ***I live in the desert, where the temperature is always the way I like it—not too hot, not too cold. I also like the colors of the desert's sunrise and sunset—they float across the sky like a rainbow. When the sun is barely going down, the pink color comes out, and the yellow blends to orange. The rainbow is like the houses around me.***
>
> **—Linda Chavaria, a student living in Tucson, from her essay "The Invisible Desert"**

The Sonoran Desert occupies the southwestern part of Arizona. This large desert extends into California and Mexico. The Sonora Desert is one of the hottest and driest deserts in North America. It is at its hottest and driest beside the Colorado River. The Sonoran Desert can be recognized by the tall, saguaro

A Gila monster pauses next to a cactus in the Sonoran Desert.

cactus and organ pipe cactus. Small trees such as mesquite and ironwood give some shade. Creosote grows in the driest lower elevations. Sprawling prickly pear, cholla cactus, and compact barrel cactus grow here too. Living among these plants are scorpions, reptiles such as rattlesnakes and gila monsters, and various birds.

Besides the Sonoran, Arizona has has three other major deserts. The Mohave is located in the northwestern part of the state. Northeastern Arizona is home to the Great Basin Desert, and the Chihuahuan Desert is located in the state's southeastern corner.

Rivers

The Colorado River is the major river of Arizona. The waters of nearly all the rivers in Arizona eventually flow into it. Among its tributaries, or smaller rivers that are connected to it, are the Little Colorado, Bill Williams, and Gila Rivers. The Gila is the second major river of Arizona. It flows east to west across southern Arizona. The Salt River and San Pedro are tributaries of the Gila.

Arizona has many small, dry rivers. They have water only after a heavy rainstorm. Often, the water flows into a dry basin and soon soaks into the ground.

Dams across the major rivers form reservoirs and artificial lakes. Water stored behind the dams is used to irrigate crops and to supply the needs of people living in the cities. Hydroelectric plants at these dams generat electricity using the power of the flowing water. Hoover Dam, on the Colorado River forms Lake Mead. It is one of the largest artificial lakes in the world. Theodore Roosevelt Dam in south-central Arizona was built in 1911 across the Salt River. The dam helped to make Arizona an important agricultural region.

The Black River flows through the San Carlos Apache Indian Reservation in eastern Arizona.

Climate

The wide range of landforms and elevations in Arizona create extremes in the weather and climate. The southwestern corner of the state receives only about four inches of rain a year—the least amount in the state. Most of the state receives ten to twenty inches of precipitation each year. The high mountains and Colorado Plateau can receive ten or more feet of snow every year. Arizona has two rainy seasons. Gentle rains fall during the winter, between December and March. The summer monsoon, between July and September, is when Arizona receives most of its annual

Threatening storm clouds brew over the Superstition Mountains in the central part of the state.

rainfall. During this time, summer storms can be quick and severe. A thunderstorm can pass through an area, hitting it with hailstones, sharp winds, and lightning. Rushing water soon floods the narrow canyons and the streets.

Arizona also has a cycle of wet years followed by years of drought. During a drought, some areas receive no rainfall at all. Farms dry out and cannot produce enough crops. Animals and livestock also suffer from the lack of water. During times of drought the danger of terrible forest fires also increases because the plants and trees are so dry.

Temperatures in the state also vary. Daytime temperatures in July can top 110 degrees Fahrenheit in southern Arizona. The state's high plateaus have a more comfortable 90-degree temperature. In January, the temperature averages in the fifties in southern Arizona. In the northern parts of the state and in the high mountains, temperatures can drop to below freezing after the sun goes down.

Wildlife

Some animals, like coyotes, cottontails, bats, bobcats, skunks, raccoons, foxes, and mule deer, live throughout Arizona. Small herds of antelope graze on the grasslands. Black bears live in the mountains. Javelinas, which look like small wild boars, roam among the cactus and mesquite. Mud turtles live in the ponds and rivers. In the desert, tortoises protect themselves from heat and cold by burrowing in the sand. Numerous snakes and lizards bask on the rocks or wait in the shade. The Gila monster, a large beaded lizard, lives in the desert. A great variety of migrating birds stop in the Chiricahua Mountains of southeastern Arizona. Arizona is also known for its beautiful butterflies.

A young javelina explores its surroundings at the Arizona-Sonora Desert Museum near Tucson.

Endangered Species

Animal and plant species become endangered when the number of individual animals or plants is reduced. This can happen when the habitat changes or is lost. Most often, natural habitats change when humans establish cities and towns or pollute the land and water. As a result of these changes, the animals may not be able to find food or safe places to hide. The plants can no longer grow there. While Arizona is a large state, the habitats of some of its animals and plants have changed too much for them. Some of Arizona's wildlife is in danger of disappearing, but many organizations and concerned residents are working together to try to help some of these endangered species.

Plants & Animals

Rattlesnake

The dull colors of rattlesnakes help them disappear into their surroundings. Eleven species of rattlesnake live in Arizona. Each of these venomous snakes has a rattle made of dried skin at the end of its tail.

Mule Deer

Mule deer get their name from their big upright ears. They live throughout Arizona, from the sparse deserts to the forested mountains. They feed on spring grasses, buds, bark, and twigs.

Pinyon Pine

The pinyon pine is one of the trees growing in the forests of the high Colorado Plateau of northern Arizona. Pinyon pines produce delicious, nutritious nuts.

Cholla Cactus

Cholla cacti grow in the sandy washes and on the gravelly mountainsides of southern Arizona. Long, sharp spines cover the cylindrical stems. On some cholla, the spines are so thick that the cactus looks fuzzy.

White-Nosed Coati

This mammal—also referred to as a coatimundi—lives in the Sonoran and Chihuahuan Deserts. It looks a lot like a raccoon and gets its name from the white fur at the tip of its snout. Coatis eat nuts, fruits, small lizards, and insects.

Black-Chinned Hummingbird

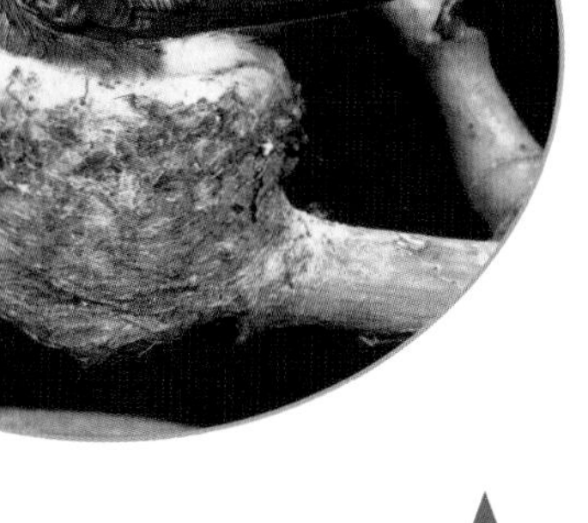

The summer rainy season draws a variety of hummingbirds to Arizona. Many of them are migrating from their nesting grounds in northwestern America to the tropical forests of Mexico and Central America. The black-chinned hummingbird likes open areas near rivers that have sycamores and cottonwoods.

The razorback sucker is a fish native to Arizona. It lives on the sandy bottom of rivers with strong currents. To spawn, or breed, it seeks quieter wetlands and backwaters. These fish used to live throughout the Gila River and its tributaries and in the Colorado River. Today only a few hundred razorback suckers live in the wild. Many of them are found in Lake Mohave, behind Davis Dam on the Colorado River. Dams have changed the river currents and the sediments on the riverbeds and prevent the razorbacks from migrating to their spawning areas. The rivers and lakes now have nonnative trout that eat razorback eggs and young. To increase the number of razorback suckers, people are raising the fish in hatcheries. When the hatchery fish are old enough, they are released into the wild, where they can live and breed with the wild fish. Scientists are hopeful that the razorback sucker will survive. Tom Pruitt, the manager of a hatchery, calls the razorback sucker "part of the heritage of this entire hemisphere."

When sucker fish populations were large, the fish could be found in lakes and rivers in Arizona, Colorado, Nevada, Utah, Wyoming, and New Mexico.

For hundreds of years jaguars have been hunted for their furs and to prevent them from eating livestock on farms.

The jaguar is another one of Arizona's endangered animals. The jaguar is the largest cat native to the western hemisphere. Most jaguars are found in parts of Mexico and Central and South America. But since Arizona borders Mexico, jaguars can sometimes be found in the state. Jaguars need a large, roadless territory, far away from people in which to roam to find food and a mate. But land development has cut into the wild spaces. For hundreds of years, jaguars have been hunted for their furs and to prevent them from eating livestock on farms. Their numbers are so low in Arizona that many scientists believe that jaguars are no longer breeding in the state. On rare occasions, a jaguar has been seen in the Baboquivari and the Peloncillo Mountains of southern Arizona. But scientists are not sure if the animal was visiting or was living in the mountains. Wildlife agencies in Arizona and New Mexico are working with officials in Mexico to preserve the jaguar's habitat and to prevent the jaguar from being killed.

2 From the Beginning

People have been living in Arizona for at least 12,000 years. Their ancestors came from Asia during the last Ice Age. At their campsites, they left stone spear points called Clovis points. They hunted large grazing animals, such as mammoth and bison, and caught small animals like rabbits. After eating and resting, they began again to search for more game and plant foods. By about 8000 B.C.E. the climate had warmed, and the large animals, except for the bison, had died out.

People in Arizona began to build houses of mud, stone, and wood. Many of the houses were round and the floor was dug into the ground. Families built their houses nearby to each other. They hunted and trapped animals and collected wild plant foods. They also planted corn, squash, beans, and cotton and kept turkeys. They scratched religious symbols onto the rocks.

Between 1 and 500 C.E., several Native American cultures arose in the deserts, mountains, and canyons of Arizona. The Anasazi—also called the Ancestral Puebloan Culture—lived in

Two Navajo boys herd their sheep in the Kaibab National Forest around 1946.

what is now northeastern Arizona and northwestern New Mexico. They are the ancestors of the Zuni and Hopi of Arizona and of the Pueblo people living in New Mexico. The Anasazi built villages in protected areas on the sides of cliffs.

The Keet Seel Ruin is Arizona's largest cliff dwelling. Similar Anasazi ruins can be found within the Navajo National Monument in northern Arizona.

Ruins of their villages are found in Canyon de Chelly. The Anasazi were part of a trade network that carried feathers, shells, salt, and turquoise to the people of the Southwest, Mexico, the Great Plains, and the western coasts.

The Hohokam lived in the southern part of present-day Arizona by the Gila and Salt Rivers. The Hohokam were expert farmers and grew a variety of crops. They built canals to bring water from the rivers to their fields. These canals have been discovered under the cities of Tucson and Phoenix. Casa Grande, a large adobe building between Phoenix and Tucson, was built by the Hohokam.

The Mogollon lived in the desert mountains of southern Arizona and New Mexico. They farmed on the narrow ledges and often moved their settlements.

By the mid 1400s, the Anasazi, Hohokam, and Mogollon had left their traditional homelands. The Anasazi moved to new regions in the late 1200s, while the Mogollon and Hohokam moved sometime around the 1300s. Experts are not sure exactly why these native peoples left the area. Droughts may have made food scarce and life harsh, forcing them to move closer to water sources such as rivers. New people may have moved into the area and crowded them out. It is also possible that they started living among the other cultures in the area.

Around this time, the Navajo and Apache had moved into the area. They came from the northern regions that include present-day Canada. At the time, the Navajo and Apache belonged to one group. When they lived in Arizona they separated. The Navajo settled among the mesas of northeastern Arizona. The Apache settled in the rugged mountains of southeastern Arizona.

Coronado and his men were not successful in finding gold in the region. The region's hot and dry conditions also made things very difficult during their expeditions.

Spanish Rule

Soldiers and missionaries (religious people who wanted to share their religion with others) from Spain arrived in Mexico in the 1520s. In 1540 Francisco Vásquez de Coronado and a large party of men left Mexico City. They traveled north in a long line of horses, cattle, and sheep. The soldiers were looking for gold and for the honor of claiming territory and wealth for Spain. They crossed the area that includes present-day Arizona and New Mexico and headed eastward to the Plains and west to find the ocean. The Spanish were disappointed. They did not find gold in the dry land and sometimes fought with the native people.

In 1691, the missionary Eusebio Francisco Kino visited the O'odham settlements in the Sonoran Desert. He started a mission at Tumacácori. He then established the San Xavier del Bac mission and many others. Father Kino traveled tirelessly among the missions. He told the native people about Christianity and taught the O'odham people European-style farming. He introduced wheat, grapes, and oranges and brought sheep, horses, mules, and cattle. The people began to keep livestock. Father Kino drew detailed maps of the region and urged the Spanish government to promote settlement of the area.

The San Xavier del Bac mission—often called the White Dove of the Desert—has been restored and preserved through the years. Visitors to the site can attend Catholic services or view the artifacts in its museum.

A miner from the Yaqui tribe found chunks of silver on a farm called Arissona near present-day Nogales. Spaniards rushed from Mexico to search for more. They dug up the ground and found more silver, but it soon ran out. Problems grew between the Native Americans and the Europeans. One group of Native Americans, the Pimas, revolted. In 1751 they killed miners, settlers, and missionaries and burned their houses and churches. To protect themselves from more attacks, the Spanish built a walled presidio, or fort, at Tubac in 1752. Soldiers stayed in the presidio and a town grew outside the adobe walls. In 1775, the Spanish government established a site for a new presidio at Tucson.

Historians are not sure of the origin of the name Arizona. It may come from a Tohono O'odham word meaning "place at the spring" or a Basque word meaning "place of the good oaks."

Mexican Rule

Just as the Americans fought the Revolutionary War to be free of British rule, Mexicans wanted independence from Spain. Mexico broke away from Spain in 1810 and after eleven years of war, it became an independent country in 1821. After the war there was little money left to help the settlers in the Arizona area. Instead, the Mexican government gave grants of land as rewards to soldiers and leaders. These lands formed big ranchos where livestock was raised. Some of the Spanish and Mexican land grants stayed with Arizona families for generations.

From 1846 to 1848 Mexico and the United States fought each other in the Mexican-American War. The Treaty of Guadalupe Hidalgo was signed on February 2, 1848, ending the war. The treaty gave much of Mexico's northern frontier to

the United States. This land included all of Arizona north of the Gila River, present-day California, Nevada, and Utah. Parts of New Mexico, Colorado, Wyoming, Oklahoma, and Kansas were also included. However, the Arizona towns of Tucson and Tubac were still in Mexico.

The United States wanted more land from Mexico to build an all-weather railroad. In 1853, Mexico agreed to the Gadsden Purchase. Mexican president Santa Anna sold the area south of the Gila River to the United States. The southern border of Arizona was set.

The first official mail service through Arizona started in 1857 and used stage coaches and mules. The mail took twenty-seven days to travel from San Antonio, Texas, through Tucson and Yuma, to San Diego, California.

In the United States

Americans crossed Arizona on their way to the gold rush in California. Ferries at Yuma took them across the Colorado River. Others stayed in Arizona to search for silver and gold or to raise cattle and grow wheat.

Arizona was a part of the Territory of New Mexico. President Abraham Lincoln signed the bill that created the Territory of Arizona on February 24, 1863. The territorial government met at Prescott, the new capital. John Goodwin was the first governor of the territory.

Two small Civil War battles occurred in Arizona. Union and Confederate troops fought at Stanwix Station, east of Yuma on March 29 or 30, 1862. They met again on April 15, 1862, at Picacho Pass, north of Tucson.

Tensions between Americans and Native Americans in the region increased. For years the

Navajo and Apache had fought with the Spanish and Mexicans. At first the native peoples welcomed the American government and settlers. They all fought together against the Mexicans. But misunderstandings and disagreements grew between the two groups. Settlers did not like some of the natives' traditional practices, which included raiding horses and cattle from the settlers' camps and ranches. In response, the settlers attacked and eventually the U.S. Army wanted to control the Native Americans.

Some native groups went to reservations or accepted food from the army. Others did all they could to resist. Kit Carson of the U.S. Army pursued the Navajo. He burned their crops, killed their sheep, and captured the hungry Navajo in Canyon de Chelly. In 1863 he sent more than 8,000 Navajo to New Mexico on what is called the Long Walk. During this 300-mile-long winter trip, hundreds of Navajos died. The Navajos that survived the journey stayed in New Mexico for nearly five years. In 1867 they were allowed to return to a reservation in Arizona.

The Apaches roamed a large area covering southern Arizona, New Mexico, and northern Mexico. After the Civil War ended in 1865, more American soldiers were available to come to Arizona to try to control the Apache. The Apache groups led by Cochise and Geronimo seemed impossible to catch. They knew their way in the mountains and would escape to Mexico where they were out of the reach of the American troops. Cochise accepted land for a reservation in 1871. Geronimo also moved to the reservation but left several times because the conditions were bad. The last time he escaped, he and a small group of Apaches managed to avoid being captured by the 5,000 American soldiers pursuing them. This lasted for about a year. In 1886, however, Geronimo surrendered, ending the Apache Wars.

Chiricahua Apache prisoners sit outside of a railroad car in Arizona. Geronimo is the third man from the right in the first row.

Progress

Despite these tensions, Arizona continued to grow and prosper. News of any discovery of silver or gold spread quickly. From the 1850s, men from Sonora and California filled the mining camps and towns. Miners collected ore from streams, surface rocks, and shallow mines. When the best and easiest ore was gone from an area, they hurried to the next silver or gold strike. Tombstone was one of these boomtowns. The prospector Ed Schieffelin found silver there in 1879. Tombstone grew rapidly into one of the biggest and most unruly towns of the West. Millions of dollars of silver were taken from the earth at Tombstone. In 1887, the mines flooded with underground water and the boom ended.

Two railroad lines were built across Arizona in the 1880s. The Southern Pacific brought in Chinese laborers to lay the tracks of the southern route. The rails reached Tucson on March 20, 1880, and the Southern Pacific's transcontinental route was completed in 1881. Two years later, the Atlantic & Pacific Railroad completed a rail line through Flagstaff and across northern Arizona. Next, short rail lines were added to the main routes. The arrival of the railroads changed Arizona. It was no longer a slow-moving, remote territory and was now connected to the western and eastern states.

Laying railroad tracks across the Arizona Territory's hot and dry land was very difficult work.

Before Arizona was served by the railroads, freighting companies traveled throughout the territory to the mines, army forts, and ranches. The wagons and pack animals carried all manner of supplies, food, mineral ores, and animal hides. This kind of travel took a long time, was expensive, and could be risky. Nevertheless, the freighting companies prospered and the profits supported other businesses. But the freighting companies could not compete with the low fees charged by the railroads and they quickly failed.

Ranches and farms were usually small. Ranchers grew enough food for themselves and sold wheat and beef to the army forts and mining camps. But eventually the large markets in California, the Midwest, and the East could be reached using the railroad. Ranchers from Texas bought acres of Arizona

A pioneer family poses on their land in the Arizona Territory in 1898.

grassland to create big cattle and sheep ranches. They loaded the animals onto trains bound for the stockyards of Kansas City.

Copper became an important resource in the 1880s. The biggest copper mines, the Copper King and the Copper Queen, were dug at Bisbee. Copper was expensive to mine and refine but it was abundant in Arizona and there was a new need to fill. American cities and factories needed copper for electric wires and machines and transportation run by electricity. The railroads made it possible to send copper ore from Arizona to the industrial centers.

Because Arizona was a territory, people living there could not vote for the United States president. They had no voting representatives in Congress, but Congress could declare any territorial law invalid. The people of Arizona wanted to be admitted to the Union. Congress gave permission in 1910 for Arizona to write a constitution. Congress and President Taft accepted the constitution and Arizona became a state on February 14, 1912.

In 1917, the United States entered World War I. Many Arizonans joined the armed forces. Others stayed in the state and produced the food and supplies needed to support the troops. Serious problems grew between the owners of the copper mines at Bisbee and the miners. On July 12, 1917, the owners directed a posse to put more than 1,000 miners on a train and sent them to New Mexico. The rest of the United States was unhappy with what had been done to the miners and condemned the mine owners.

During the 1920s and 1930s Arizona suffered along with the rest of the country during the Great Depression. The state eventually began to redevelop its economy and

bounce back. Irrigation projects allowed agriculture to expand. The state benefited from government construction projects such as dams and highways. Tourism grew, too. Arizona was promoted as a healthful place to take a vacation or spend the winter. Health seekers hoped that the dry climate would ease lung problems such as asthma and tuberculosis.

During World War II, the U.S. military used the open spaces of Arizona to train pilots. Factories produced aircraft, and the mines supplied minerals needed by the defense industries. The military and the defense industries gave the Arizona economy a boost.

During the World Wars, more women started working alongside men in the factories.

After the war, the military and defense industries stayed in Arizona. The Motorola company set up an electronics plant in Phoenix in 1948. Thousands of people were moving to Arizona and the economy was booming. The comfort of air conditioning turned Arizona into a desirable place for people and businesses to relocate. Real estate developers built communities planned

An aerial view shows a circular neighborhood in central Arizona's Sun City.

especially to appeal to retired people. Sun City, one of the first of these communities, opened west of Phoenix in 1960.

However, Arizona's progress and growth have put a strain on some of its natural resources. People have long recognized the importance of water to Arizona. The historian Thomas E. Sheridan wrote, "Without water, the land was useless." But agriculture, manufacturing, and the cities placed high demands on the water supply. Arizona has two main sources of water. Surface water is taken from rivers and the lakes formed by dams, while groundwater is pumped out from underground natural reservoirs. It has taken millions of years for the underground water to accumulate, and Arizona is taking out more groundwater than is being put in. In some places in Phoenix so much groundwater was removed that big cracks opened in the earth.

Arizona, California, Colorado, Nevada, New Mexico, Wyoming, Utah, and Mexico share the water of the Colorado River. Arizona wanted to route its share to where most people live and where it is most needed. In 1968 President Lyndon Johnson approved the Central Arizona Project, or CAP. This is an enormous water project that brings Colorado River water to central Arizona. The system of aqueducts, tunnels, and pumping stations is 336 miles long. It reaches from Lake Havasu to the San Xavier Indian Reservation south of Tucson. Construction began in 1973. In 1985 the first water was pumped through CAP to agricultural fields near Phoenix. CAP water was delivered to Tucson in 1992.

Since more surface water has become available, less groundwater is being removed. But still it is too much. Arizonans are exploring ways to balance their water needs and

the supply. This is just one example of how Arizonans continue to adjust to the changing times and find ways to help the state progress.

An aqueduct carrying much-needed water stretches across Arizona's desert.

Important Dates

12,000 B.C.E. Paleo Indians live in Arizona.

1100s C.E. Hopi people build Oraibi village. Anasazi build cliff dwellings in Canyon de Chelly.

1300s-1500s Navajos and Apaches begin moving into the Southwest.

1350 Hohokam build Casa Grande in the Gila River valley.

1540s Francisco Vásquez de Coronado and his men explore the region.

1687 Father Eusebio Francisco Kino begins missionary work among the O'odham.

1752 Spain establishes a presidio at Tubac, the first permanent European settlement in Arizona.

John Wesley Powell

1821 Mexico gains independence from Spain.

1848 The Treaty of Guadalupe Hidalgo gives most of present-day Arizona to the United States.

1853 Through the Gadsden Purchase the United States buys from Mexico the area south of the Gila River.

1863 President Abraham Lincoln declares Arizona a territory.

1864 Navajo are driven from their homeland and endure the Long Walk. They are permitted to return in 1867.

1869 John Wesley Powell explores the Colorado River.

1881 Southern Pacific Railroad crosses southern Arizona.

Theodore Roosevelt Dam

1886 Geronimo surrenders to the U.S. Army and the Apache Wars end.

1911 The Theodore Roosevelt Dam, on the Salt River, is completed.

1912 Arizona becomes the forty-eighth state on February 14.

1922 Colorado River Compact divides the Colorado River's water among seven states, including Arizona.

1950s Air conditioning is widely used in houses, factories, and businesses.

1960 Sun City, one of the first retirement communities, opens.

1968 The Central Arizona Project is approved. The plan includes the building of canals, pipelines, and tunnels to bring Colorado River water to central Arizona.

2000 The U.S. Census shows that over the last decade Arizona's population has grown by 40 percent.

2001 Arizona Diamondbacks win the World Series.

3 The People

For at least 12,000 years, people have been moving into and through Arizona. They have come looking for a good place to live, to farm, and to work. Every ten years the federal government takes a census, which is a count of everyone living in the United States. The last census was taken in 2000 and counted 5,130, 632 people living in Arizona. The two largest counties are Maricopa County and Pima County. Phoenix is the state's largest city. It is a part of Maricopa County and has a population of 1,321,045 people. The second-largest city is Tucson, which is in Pima County and has 486,699 people. Other large cities are Mesa, Glendale, Scottsdale, Chandler, and Tempe. But Arizona also has many towns. Some are small and have a few thousand or a few hundred residents. Some towns are even smaller.

The census also counts people according to their race. Like the rest of the United States, Arizona is approximately seventy-five percent white. Through Arizona's history, most of the white people who settled the area were of European descent. They immigrated from countries like England, Ireland, France,

A father and son work on their ranch in Cochise County.

More than 400,000 people make Tucson their home. Many others live outside the city, but drive in to work in its thriving businesses.

Germany, or Italy. Other white residents included Americans from other parts of the United States.

Other racial groups form small percentages of the population. African Americans make up about 3 percent of the state's population. Arizona's population is only 1.8 percent Asian. Five percent of the population is Native American. In the census about 25 percent of Arizona's population lists themselves as being of Hispanic or Latino origin. This means that they or their ancestors came from a Spanish-speaking nation. Most Arizona Latinos trace their roots to Mexico. Others have arrived from Guatemala, El Salvador, Colombia, Peru, and other countries in Central America and South America.

Native Americans

Arizona is home to seventeen Native American tribes. These nations have lived in the same area for hundreds of years. Today, the Native American nations in Arizona control more than one quarter of the state's land. Most of Arizona's Native Americans live on reservations. Others live off of the reservation, in Arizona's cities and towns.

The Navajo Nation is in the northeast corner of Arizona and spills over into New Mexico and Utah. It is the largest Native American nation in the United States. It has the most members

Navajo girls in traditional dress prepare to dance at a powwow on the Navajo reservation.

and the most land. The Tohono O'odham Nation is also large. Its land is divided into four areas in southern Arizona. Other tribes include the Hopi, San Carlos Apache, White Mountain Apache, and Yavapai. The Hopi Nation's land is surrounded by the Navajo Nation's property.

The tribes govern themselves. They choose their own leaders, write their own laws, and operate businesses to bring in money. The Ak-Chin Indian Community and the Gila River Indian Community use their land for agriculture. The Navajo and Hopi Nations mine coal. Many reservations are open to tourists. They invite visitors to enjoy the recreation spots and areas of natural beauty. The biggest money-maker for the tribes has been the gaming casinos. The tribes use the money brought in by the casinos to build houses, schools, health clinics, and community centers. The money is also used to pay for the police and fire departments on the reservations.

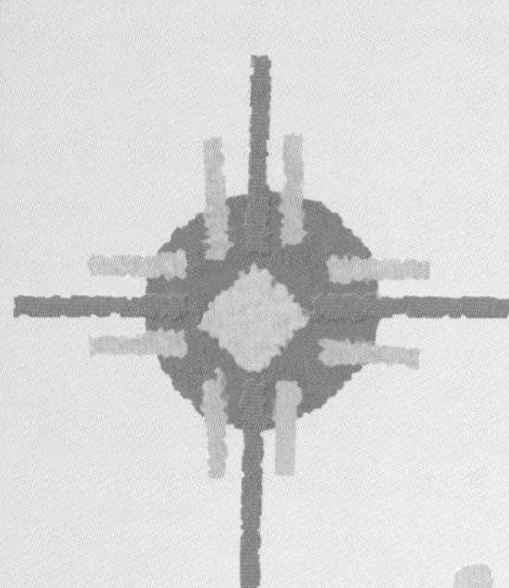

Create a Navajo Sandpainting

Sandpainting is a traditional art used by the Navajo. After a healing ceremony, sandpaintings were destroyed to symbolize destroying the illness. Today, Navajo artists paint with sand to make lasting art. Using colored sand and crushed rock, they paint landscapes or drawings that tell a story. Much of this artwork includes traditional designs such as spiders, snakes, people, bears, turtles, corn, clouds, lightning, sun, rain, and rainbows.

What You Need

Heavy paper or a smooth piece of plywood
Clear glue
Paintbrushes
Newspaper
Colored sand (purchase from craft store, or make your own)

To make colored sand, you will need

3 cups of sand
Plastic bags
Food coloring
Rubber or latex gloves

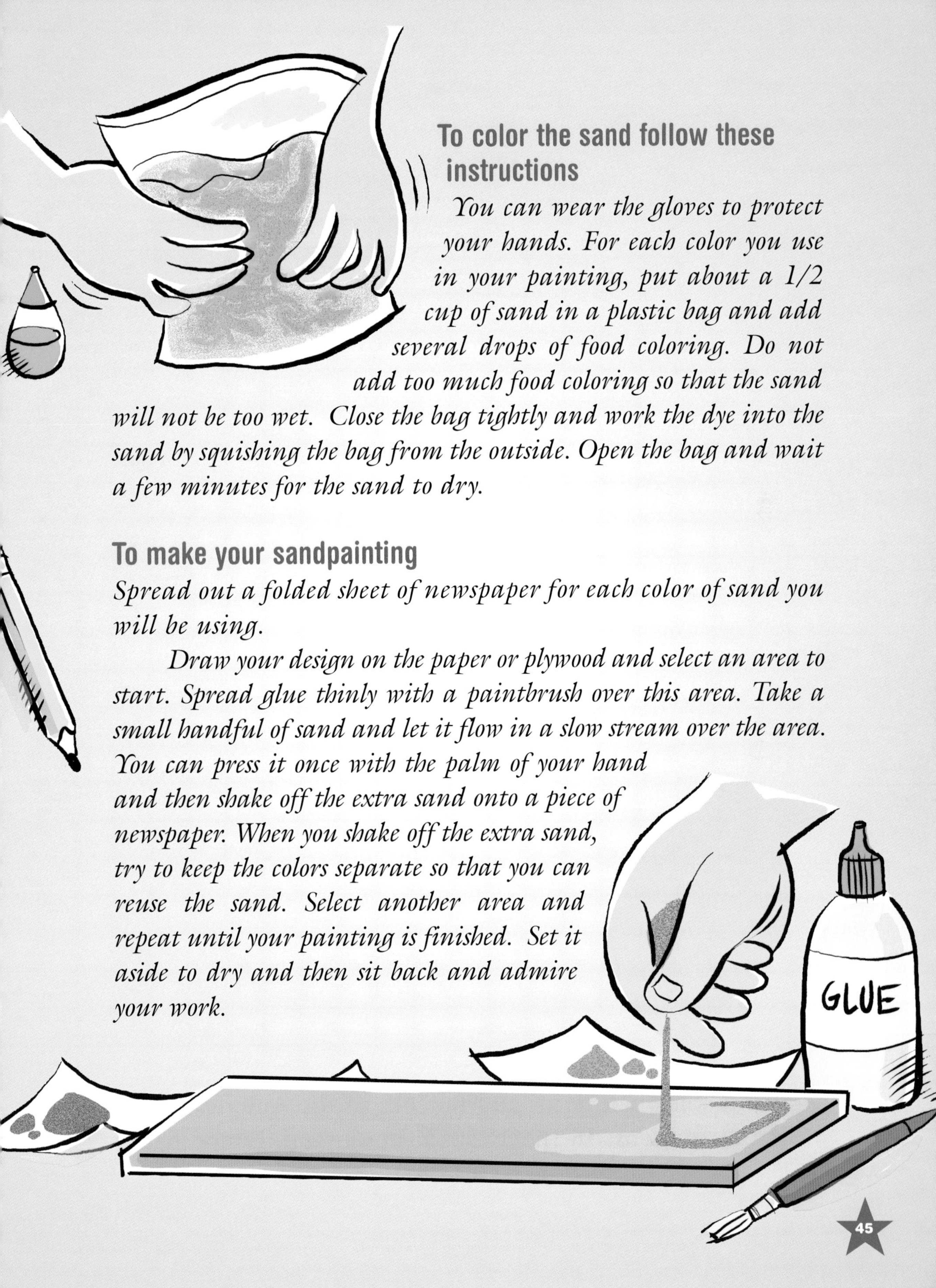

To color the sand follow these instructions

You can wear the gloves to protect your hands. For each color you use in your painting, put about a 1/2 cup of sand in a plastic bag and add several drops of food coloring. Do not add too much food coloring so that the sand will not be too wet. Close the bag tightly and work the dye into the sand by squishing the bag from the outside. Open the bag and wait a few minutes for the sand to dry.

To make your sandpainting

Spread out a folded sheet of newspaper for each color of sand you will be using.

Draw your design on the paper or plywood and select an area to start. Spread glue thinly with a paintbrush over this area. Take a small handful of sand and let it flow in a slow stream over the area. You can press it once with the palm of your hand and then shake off the extra sand onto a piece of newspaper. When you shake off the extra sand, try to keep the colors separate so that you can reuse the sand. Select another area and repeat until your painting is finished. Set it aside to dry and then sit back and admire your work.

Native Americans are dedicated to their communities and cultures. Community buildings at the Navajo Nation use modern materials but follow the traditional, symbolic shapes. Young people know about American culture but learn their own language and ceremonies too. Many Native American nations give scholarships to students so they can attend college. "Educational success is a huge priority," said Lisa Sandoval, the higher education director for the Yavapai Apache Nation.

> *I am interested in learning more about my heritage and the other tribes that live in Arizona.*
>
> —Jennifer Ben, a Navajo student

Mexican Americans and Latinos

Arizona used to be part of Mexico, and now Arizona and Mexico share a border. So it is not surprising that Spanish-speaking people have long been part of the culture of Arizona. Spanish is widely spoken and read in southern Arizona. Towns, mountains, and landmarks have Spanish names.

When the Southwest passed to the United States in 1848, there were many Mexican families living there. They had farms and ranches along the Salt River and Gila River. They dug irrigation ditches to bring water to the fields and orchards where they grew wheat, hay, and fruit. People in the Mexican state of Sonora were expert miners. When they heard about the gold discoveries in Arizona they moved north to mine the gold. During the territorial period, more Mexicans settled in southern Arizona. Americans came too and many Mexicans sold their farms and ranches to the Americans and moved into towns. In the 1880s, Tucson and Tempe had a

A traditional Mexican dance troupe performs in front of the state capitol during a statehood celebration.

majority of Latino residents. Mexican Americans were civic and business leaders. They were active in politics and many were elected to the territorial legislature.

In the 1900s, however, Mexican Americans often faced discrimination and poor treatment. Children had to attend separate schools. Mexican-American workers were not always able to find work or fair wages. They joined labor unions to improve their work situation. "Even in church, there was segregation," recalled Josie Ortega Sanchez of Tempe. In the 1950s the organization Alianza Hispano-Americana fought for integration. In the 1960s, Mexican-American youth formed new organizations and called themselves Chicanos. They demanded that the civil rights of Chicanos and Latinos be recognized. Latinos and Chicanos have since regained an influential role in education, politics, and business in Arizona. The Latino and Chicano population in Arizona is growing rapidly. People think that some day it will make up the majority of the state's population.

Asians

Chinese people began to arrive in Arizona in the 1850s. Like the other prospectors, they were looking for gold and silver. In the mines, they did dangerous and dirty work and were paid very low wages. In the towns and mining camps they endured hatred and abuse. In the 1870s and 1880s the railroads brought Chinese laborers to Arizona. It was hard work to prepare the rail beds and lay the tracks. Wages for the Chinese were lower than what was paid to the white workers. After the boom of the mines ended and the railroads were completed, most Chinese left Arizona. The few who stayed opened businesses or started farms.

Japanese people came into Arizona in the late 1890s and early 1900s. They faced discrimination and attacks by whites and by Mexican Americans. Congress passed laws that ended immigration by Chinese and Japanese people. Arizona passed laws that restricted whom these Asian residents could marry and where they could live.

After World War II, Asian Americans became better accepted in Arizona. In 1946, voters elected Wing F. Ong to the state's House of Representatives. He was the first Chinese American to sit on any state legislature.

During World War II, Japan and the United States were enemies. The U.S. government was afraid that Japanese Americans would help Japan. The government confined many Japanese Americans living in California and Washington to internment camps far from their homes. Two of these camps were in Arizona. Many of the internees sent to the camps were American citizens who had been born in the United States. They were forced to leave their jobs, their homes, and most of their belongings. Near the end of the war, the United

Japanese Americans visit the Poston Relocation Center. These men and their families were interned in Arizona during World War II.

States released the interned Japanese Americans. A few of them stayed in Arizona and tried to start over.

Recently, more Asians have moved to the state. Today nearly 100,000 Asians and Asian Americans live there. They represent many nations, including China, Japan, India, Thailand, Cambodia, and Vietnam. Asians and Asian Americans in Arizona hold a variety of jobs in different fields.

Famous Arizonans

George W. P. Hunt: Governor

George W. P. Hunt was born in Missouri in 1859 and worked in the West as a miner and prospector. He arrived in Globe, Arizona, in 1881 where he worked for a large silver mine and eventually became president of the company. In 1910 he was elected president of the convention charged with writing a constitution for Arizona. When Arizona became a state, Hunt was elected as the first governor. He served seven terms as governor. Hunt died in Phoenix in 1934.

Kerri Strug: Olympic Gymnast

Kerri Strug grew up in Tucson and started competing in gymnastics at the age of eight. In 1992 she was the youngest U.S. athlete at the Olympics. Despite injuries and other difficulties, Strug continued to train and compete, winning many titles and medals. During the 1996 Olympics, Strug was injured, but helped her team win its first gold medal ever. For her courage, Strug received the Olympic Spirit Award.

Lorna Lockwood: State Supreme Court Chief Justice

Lorna Lockwood was born in 1903. She graduated from the University of Arizona in 1923 and from its college of law in 1925. She worked as an attorney and in 1939 was elected to the Arizona House of Representatives. She was elected to the Arizona Supreme Court in 1961. When the other justices of the court chose her to be the chief justice in 1965, she became the first woman to ever serve as a chief justice in a state supreme court.

Lewis Tewanima: Olympic Athlete

Lewis Tewanima was born on the Hopi Reservation in the late 1870s. He attended the Carlisle Indian Industrial School in Pennsylvania and trained with other great athletes. His skills as a long-distance runner impressed everyone. Tewanima was a member of the United States Olympic teams in 1908 and 1912. In the 1912 Olympic Games, he ran in the 10,000-meter race and won the silver medal.

Sharlot Hall: Writer and Historian

Sharlot Hall moved to Arizona with her family in 1882, when she was twelve years old. Hall loved Arizona and wanted to make sure that its history was preserved. She traveled through the territory to collect oral histories from the old settlers and to save Native American and pioneer artifacts. From 1909 to 1912, she served as the territorial historian. In 1928 she moved to Prescott, restored the log building that had been the territory's first capitol and governor's mansion, and used the mansion as a museum of Arizona history.

Charles Mingus: Musician

Mingus was born in Nogales in 1922. He was a talented pianist and bass player. As a composer and band leader, he reached for energetic rhythms, unexpected harmonies, and deep emotion. From the 1950s through the 1970s Mingus played alongside other respected musicians and recorded many ground-breaking albums. Charles Mingus died in 1979.

MLK Praise Dancers perform in Phoenix during a Martin Luther King Jr. Day celebration.

African Americans

African Americans were among the settlers who came west in the 1800s. In Arizona, they sought a place where they could live and raise their families without the threats of slavery. They started homesteads and ranches and worked a variety of jobs. They prospected for gold and silver and worked for the railroads. Some African Americans were cowboys and rode across the range. Others started their own businesses, such as barbershops and restaurants.

But African Americans did not have an easy time living in Arizona during the early 1900s. School segregation was made legal in 1909. This meant that African-American children had separate schools from white children. Most African Americans were restricted to living in certain neighborhoods. It was difficult for many to get a good education or a well-paying job. To end racial hatred and to change the laws, African Americans formed clubs and organizations. They held demonstrations and sit-ins. In 1951, the Tucson schools were desegregated. The state Civil Rights Act was passed in 1965. African Americans began to be elected to local and state offices. In Arizona today African Americans are a vital part of their communities. Many are successful businesspeople, lawyers, educators, doctors, and legislators.

Arizona's Growth

Since Arizona became a state, each census has shown it to have a high rate of growth. From 1990 to 2000, Arizona's population grew by 40 percent. This makes Arizona the second-fastest growing state, after Nevada. Many experts expect Arizona to continue to grow at a high rate for some time.

Why do so many people move to Arizona? For many businesses, it is not too expensive to build factories and run offices in Arizona. As a result, many people move to Arizona to work at these businesses. People also enjoy the state's natural beauty and the pleasant climate. They are attracted by the promise of work and reasonably priced homes. Many people move to Arizona to be near their families who already live there. A number of retired people move to Arizona to relax and enjoy quiet living. No matter their background or the reasons why they move to the state, it is clear that many people believe that Arizona has much to offer.

A young Arizonan takes a quiet moment to sit outside and read.

Calendar of Events

Yuma Lettuce Days

Yuma County is an agricultural region with a productive, winter growing season. In January, the town of Yuma celebrates itself as the Lettuce Capital of the World with displays of head lettuce, leaf lettuce, romaine, and winter produce.

Tucson Gem and Mineral Show

People come to Tucson in February to admire and trade gems and minerals that have been collected from all over the world.

Cactus League Baseball

During spring training in March, major league baseball teams warm up in Arizona. Fans attend preseason games in Tucson and Phoenix.

Tucson International Mariachi Conference

Mariachi music has traveled from Mexico and into the cities of the United States. Sharply-dressed bands present their songs in concerts, workshops, and a fiesta in April.

Waila Festival

Waila is a Tohono O'odham word derived from the Spanish word *baile*, to dance. In May the Tohono O'odham gather in Tucson to enjoy Waila, a partner dance blending European and Mexican music and steps.

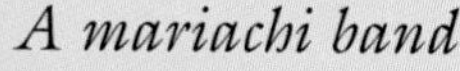

A mariachi band

July Fourth in Bisbee

The national holiday is observed in Bisbee with the traditional July Fourth parade, foot races, and fireworks. The mucking and drilling contests recall Bisbee's past as a booming mining town.

World's Oldest Continuous Rodeo

Cowboys and cowgirls meet in Payson to test their roping and riding skills. Children try mutton-busting, roping a running sheep. The rodeo has been held every August since 1884.

Navajo Nation Fair at Window Rock

During the week-long fair in September, the Navajo people share their arts, crafts, and foods and hold dances, contests, a parade, a rodeo, and a powwow.

Arizona State Fair

Arizonans come to Phoenix in October for the state fair. There are science, farm, and animal exhibits; shows and concerts; and exciting rides and races.

El Tour de Tucson

Thousands of cyclists compete in November in 111-, 75-, 50-, and 31-mile races on the roads that encircle Tucson.

Bull riding at a rodeo

4 How It Works

In Arizona, there are several overlapping governments: the federal, state, county, city, and tribal governments. The state follows federal—or national—laws set down by the United States government. But the state's own government also sets up laws and standards that residents must follow.

The state is divided into fifteen counties. Each county is led by a board of supervisors. Counties are made up of cities and towns. Arizona's cities and towns are headed by mayors and city councils. County and city governments deal with local issues. Such issues include zoning problems, city or town budgets, and public school issues.

Arizonans are represented in the U.S. Senate by two senators and in the U.S. House of Representatives by six congress members.

State Government

The constitution of Arizona went into effect when Arizona became a state in 1912. It is the basic law of Arizona. It guarantees the legal rights enjoyed by each person in the state. It describes how the state government is organized and what it does. The state government

A white statue sits atop the dome of the Arizona capitol, where the state government once met. The dome is made of copper in honor of mining's great contributions to Arizona's history and economy.

is divided into three departments, the legislative, the executive, and the judicial. Each department has its own areas of responsibility, yet they also work together. The officials of the state government meet and work in Phoenix, the state capital.

Branches of Government

Executive The executive branch includes the governor, secretary of state, state treasurer, attorney general, and superintendent of public education. The governor is the chief executive of the state. With the other executive officers, the governor conducts the business of the state and enforces its laws.

Legislative The Arizona legislature has two chambers: the senate and the house of representatives. The senate has thirty members and the house of representatives has sixty members. The senators and representatives write and vote on bills, or proposals for new laws. They also plan the state budget.

Judicial The judicial branch includes the state's courts and judges. Every city has a municipal court. Every county has a justice of the peace court and a superior court. The state also has a court of appeals where people can argue the fairness of a previous decision. The state supreme court is the highest court in Arizona. It creates the rules followed by all the courts, judges, and attorneys in the state.

Citizen Lawmakers

In Arizona, private citizens are also lawmakers. Voters have the power of the initiative, referendum, and recall at the state level and in their cities and counties. In an initiative, voters propose a new law or an amendment to the state constitution. They collect signatures to have the initiative placed on the ballot. At election time, people vote for or against the new law or amendment. In a referendum people vote on whether a current law should remain in effect. If people are unhappy with how

Voting has been important to Arizonans for a long time. This photograph shows residents voting in territorial elections in 1906.

an elected official is representing them, they may vote to recall, or remove, the official from office. Brent W. Brown, associate professor of political science at Arizona State University calls the initiative, referendum, and recall provisions "a major force in the state's political environment."

How a Bill Becomes Law

The territorial capital was established at Prescott in 1864. It was moved to Tucson in 1867 and back to Prescott in 1877. Phoenix became the capital in 1899 and remained so when Arizona became a state.

When an idea for a law is first proposed, it is called a bill. Senators and representatives always look for ideas for bills. Often these ideas are suggested by state citizens. But only elected legislators may officially introduce a bill. The bill is introduced to the senate or the house. A bill introduced in the senate first travels through the senate, and a bill introduced in the house of representatives first travels through the house.

After the bill is introduced, it is assigned to a committee for study. The committee suggests ways to improve the bill. If the committee does not think the bill is worthwhile, they let it "die." If the committee likes the proposal, the bill goes to the Legislative Council. The Legislative Council is a committee of senators, representatives, and staff attorneys. The council carefully studies whether the bill conflicts in any way with an existing law, including the state constitution. The Legislative Council then writes a draft of the bill in legal language.

At this point, the bill is ready to be formally presented to the senate or house of representatives. The title of the bill is read aloud and the bill is given a number. After the first reading the bill has a second reading and is assigned to a committee.

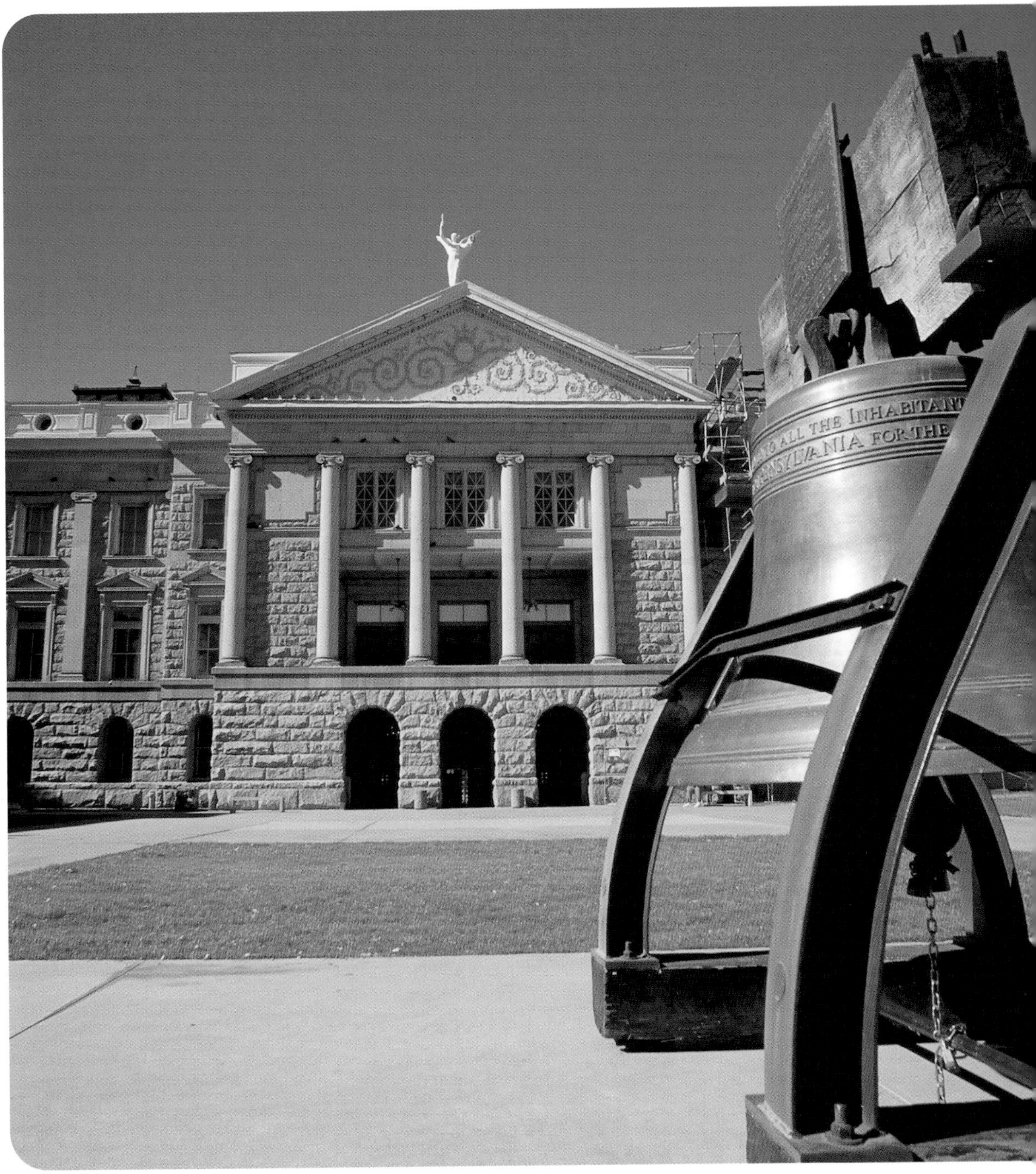

In the past, the governor's office, both legislative houses, and the state supreme court were located in the capitol building. Today, however, the building is the Arizona Capitol Museum.

This committee again examines the bill to understand the benefits and effects of the bill. The committee often holds public hearings. People speak before the committee and explain how the bill will be helpful or harmful. The committee may decide that the bill needs to be changed and will add amendments to the bill. The committee votes to recommend the bill to the house or senate. If the bill has passed the committee and made it to the senate or the house, the legislators debate the bill. Then they vote on whether or not to approve the bill. When the bill is approved it is sent to the other legislative house and the process is repeated.

Once the bill has passed in both the senate and the house of representatives, it is sent to the governor. If he or she approves the bill, it becomes a law. Sometimes the governor does not think a bill will be good for the state. He or she will then veto—reject—the bill. The legislators can vote again on the bill. If two thirds of the members of each house vote "yes" on the bill then they have succeeded in overriding the governor's veto. The bill becomes a law even without the governor's signature.

Two justices of the United States Supreme Court have practiced law in Arizona. William Rehnquist was appointed to the Supreme Court in 1971. In 1986 he became the Chief Justice of the Supreme Court. Sandra Day O'Connor was appointed to the U.S. Supreme Court in 1981.

You Make a Difference

A government that is served by elected leaders and lawmakers needs voters. Many Arizona citizens are concerned about their states and take the time to understand the issues before voting. To increase the number of voters, a program called

Kids Voting Arizona was developed. In this program, children and teenagers are helping adults to vote by setting an example. In school they learn about the democratic process. At home they are encouraged to discuss politics with their families. The discussion often gets the adults interested in learning about the candidates and what they stand for. By election day both the children and the adults know who they want to vote for. They go together to the polling place in their neighborhood. Children go into the voting booth and mark their votes on a "kid's" ballot while the adults use an official ballot. This program has helped to bring more adults to the polls and has helped children learn about the voting process.

You may want to write to Arizona's state senators or representatives. A map of Arizona is found at this Web site: http://www.azleg.state.az.us/maps/state.htm By clicking on the region in which you live, you can find out who your representatives and senators are. Their email addresses and phone numbers are also provided. Your legislators have offices nearby in your town or county too. Look in the telephone book for these in the "Government" section.

5 Making a Living

The people of Arizona are skillful and resourceful when it comes to making a living. They follow the traditional activities of farming, mining, and raising livestock. They also keep their ideas fresh and are open to trying new technologies and markets for their services and products.

Agriculture

Irrigation has made Arizona into an important agricultural state. The state has day after day of sunshine and a nearly year-round growing season. The land of southern Arizona along the Gila River and in the west along the Colorado River is given to huge fields of vegetables, citrus fruit, and cotton. Many leafy green crops such as lettuce do especially well in the mild winter of the low desert.

Arizona is known for five "Cs"—copper, citrus, cotton, cattle, and climate.

Arizona farms produce lettuce, lemons, broccoli, cauliflower, cantaloupe, and honeydew melons. Citrus groves are planted with lemons, grapefruit, oranges, and

A tourist admires the sandstone formations in Paria Canyon-Vermillion Cliffs Wilderness Area.

tangerines. The fruit is sold fresh or processed for frozen juice concentrate. Arizona also grows carrots, potatoes, spinach, onions, parsley, and bok choy.

A worker harvests broccoli on a farm in Yuma.

Recipe for Citrus Ice Cream

Many Arizona farms produce juicy citrus fruits such as oranges and lemons. Here is a recipe for making a sweet and tangy dessert that is perfect throughout the year.

Ingredients:

3 1/4 cups of sugar
2 lemons
4 oranges
3 cups of milk
3 cups of whipping cream

Carefully squeeze the juice from the lemons and oranges into a large container. Be sure to strain out any pulp or seeds that might be mixed in. Ask an adult to help you squeeze out all of the juice.

In a large mixing bowl, combine the lemon and orange juice with the sugar. Stir the mixture thoroughly making sure that all the sugar gets wet.

Add the cream and milk, stirring constantly to make sure that everything mixes well.

Pour your mixture into a freezer-safe container and store it in the freezer for at least four hours. When your ice cream is ready you can eat it in a bowl, in a cone, or with some cake and cookies.

A Navajo woman herds her family's sheep along the grounds of the Navajo National Monument.

The hot climate is good for growing cotton. Cotton is the state's most profitable crop. To adjust to the different demands and changes in the economy, many cotton farmers use new technologies and growing strategies for their crops.

Arizona's lands are also used to raise livestock. Ranchers keep alive the Old West tradition of breeding cattle, sheep, and goats. Arizona's grasslands are ideal places for herds of cattle and sheep to graze. The Navajo raise Angora goats for the soft mohair.

Minerals and Resources

Arizona's ancient volcanoes have left the land rich with valuable minerals. Lush forests that once grew years ago when the climate was wetter have been transformed into coal beds and pockets of oil and natural gas.

More than one hundred mines operate in Arizona. They collect copper, molybdenum, silver, gemstones, and sand and gravel from the earth. Deep underground tunnels are dug to reach the buried deposits. When the minerals lie near the surface a mining company simply digs a big hole. An open pit mine (as the

big hole is called) is operated at Morenci by Phelps Dodge Corporation. It is the largest copper-producing site in North America. Copper is the most plentiful and valuable mineral found in Arizona. Molybdenum and silver are collected as a byproduct when copper ores are refined. Copper has many uses in electronics and in alloys. Molybdenum is an important lubricant and an ingredient in steel.

Arizona has other natural resources that are not below the ground. The high mountains of eastern Arizona support many acres of pine forests. These forests are harvested for timber. Arizona's waterways are also an important resource. Dams that have been built across the state store about a four-year supply of water. Hydroelectric plants built alongside the dams also generate electricity used by Arizonans.

Manufacturing

Arizona is a center for the research and manufacture of semiconductors. These electronic components are essential to computers, communications networks, and electronic gadgets. The state is among the world's leaders in the production of cell phones.

The plastics industry in Arizona is growing to meet the great demand for plastic products. Manufacturers use molds to shape plastic into lightweight, strong cases for cell phones, pagers, laptop and desktop computers, and electronic organizers. Arizona's plastics industry also makes disposable medical supplies and produces parts and coatings for airplanes and missiles.

The aerospace industry came to Arizona during World War II. Aircraft companies today make engines and controls for military, commercial, and private jets. They also develop missile systems for the military.

Products & Resources

Lemons

Spanish missionaries planted lemons in Arizona. Growers now produce a variety of lemons in sunny, irrigated groves east of the Colorado River. Lemons grown in Arizona are sold throughout the United States and exported to countries such as China.

Construction

Construction workers build new neighborhoods for the many people moving to Arizona. They build houses, schools, stores, industrial parks, civic centers, and stadiums. Besides creating useful structures, the construction industry employs many Arizonans.

Semiconductors

Semiconductors (sometimes called computer chips) are some of the products designed and manufactured in Arizona. Information in the form of electronic signals passes through the semiconductors. Semiconductors are used in computers, communications networks, wireless phones, and cars.

Copper

Arizona is the world's second-richest copper region of the world. Copper ores are mined and refined in Arizona. Copper is mixed with other metals to make strong, flexible alloys. Arizona copper is used in electrical wiring and in all kinds of appliances and hardware. A car has about fifty pounds of copper, and all gold jewelry contains a small amount of copper.

Tourism

Visitors come to Arizona to enjoy the natural beauty and to learn about Native American cultures. Especially in the winter, visitors go to Arizona resorts to relax and play golf. The lakes attract boaters and fishermen.

Aerospace

Aerospace companies in Arizona design and build airplanes, jets, and military missiles. They also supply many of the parts, devices, and sensors that go into aircraft. Some companies even build the black boxes that record the details of an airplane's flight.

Star trails can be seen above the telescope domes at the Kitt Peak Observatory.

Science and Technology

Astronomers come to Arizona to study the sun, stars, and planets. They find that the dry air and the elevation are ideal for observing space. Some telescopes use mirrors and lenses to collect visible light. Other telescopes detect radio signals and microwaves. Several telescopes make up the Kitt Peak National Observatory in the Baboquivari Mountains west of Tucson. The Smithsonian Institution operates the Whipple Observatory on Mount Hopkins south of Tucson. Another collection of telescopes is stationed at the Mount Graham International Observatory, northeast of Tucson. The U.S. Naval Observatory in the mountains of Flagstaff uses instruments and measurements to determine the precise time. Observations at the Lowell Observatory, also at Flagstaff, led to the discovery of the planet Pluto in 1930.

Arizona is also becoming known for its biotechnology industry. Biotechnology uses the molecular ingredients of living things to make medicines and medical devices and to improve agriculture. Biotechnology brings together the skills and knowledge of many scientific specialists. Civic leaders, businesspeople, scientists, and research centers and universities are working together to develop this exciting industry in Arizona.

Trade and Transportation

Arizona is at a transportation hub. Highways cross the state and domestic and international flights land at the airports in Phoenix, Tucson, and Yuma. Arizona is placed at a crossroad between the western and eastern United States and between the United States and Mexico.

Long before the arrival of the Europeans, the people living in Arizona carried on trade with the people living to the south in Mexico. Arizona is still part of a trade and commercial network with Mexico. Since the North American Free Trade Agreement went into effect in 1994 trade through Arizona has increased. Many of the goods traveling between Mexico and the United States pass through Tucson. Business people in Tucson hope that their region will become an even more active trading hub for Mexico and the southern United States.

Service

Everyone needs to buy groceries, clothes, personal items, and things for the house, car, and their pets. It is not surprising that grocery stores and discount retail stores are among Arizona's largest employers.

Tourism is another important part of the service industry. The tourism industry includes airports, restaurants, motels and resorts, organized tours, and car and boat rentals. Arizona tourism creates jobs for more than 110,000 people. Arizona has a range of features and landmarks that bring visitors from other states and nations. Visitors like outdoor activities such as bicycling, hiking, hunting, fishing, and boating. They search for marvelous landforms and colors and look for archaeological sites and reminders of the Old West. They come for annual celebrations

Tourists ride in an old-fashioned stage coach along Allen Street in Tombstone.

and sports tournaments. A number of visitors come from Mexico to spend a day enjoying Arizona's sites and shopping in the state's stores.

Many people in Arizona work in jobs that serve their community. They work in the offices of their city or county or are employed by state agencies. Numerous Arizonans teach in the schools or work as police officers. Rangers watch over the state and national parks and share their knowledge of the plants and animals with visitors.

The United States military is a major employer in Arizona. The Air Force, Army, and Marine Corps have bases and air stations in Arizona where pilots and soldiers practice and train. The activities at the bases are supported by many civilian (non-military) employees and suppliers. About 83,000 people are employed at military installations in Arizona.

Arizona relies on its growing industries and its hardworking residents. Working together to adjust to changing times, Arizonans continue to strive to be the best and make their state successful.

The colors of the flag of Arizona recall the history of the state. The red and yellow rays in the upper half of the flag represent the red and yellow flags carried by the Spanish explorers. The blue of the lower half is the same as the blue of the United States flag. The copper-colored star in the middle commemorates Arizona as the largest producer of copper in the nation. The red and yellow rays have the effect of the sun setting on the western horizon and show that Arizona is a western state. The flag was designed by Colonel Charles W. Harris and adopted in 1917.

The state seal is in the shape of a shield. It shows the sun rising between the mountains. On the right side, there is a dam, a reservoir, irrigated fields, and cattle. To the left, a miner stands in front of a quartz mill. The motto at the top, "Ditat Deus," means "God enriches." A circular band bearing the words "Great Seal of the State of Arizona" surrounds the seal. The date 1912 is the year that Arizona became a state.

ARIZONA

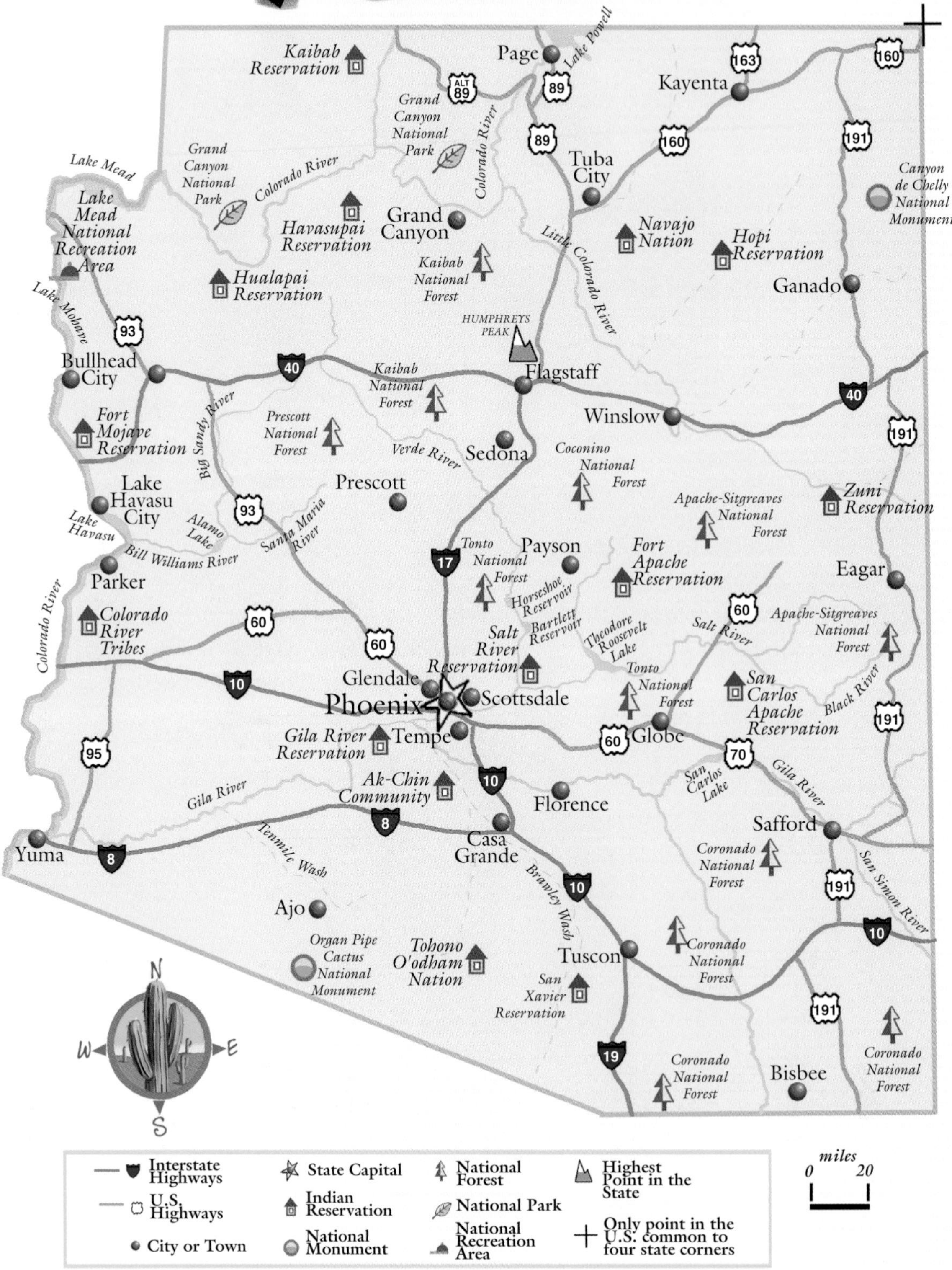

Kaibab Reservation
Page
Lake Powell
ALT 89
89
163
Kayenta
160
Grand Canyon National Park
Colorado River
89
160
191
Lake Mead
Grand Canyon National Park
Colorado River
Tuba City
Canyon de Chelly National Monument
Lake Mead National Recreation Area
Grand Canyon
Havasupai Reservation
Little Colorado River
Navajo Nation
Hopi Reservation
Kaibab National Forest
Hualapai Reservation
Ganado
Lake Mohave
93
HUMPHREYS PEAK
Bullhead City
40
Kaibab National Forest
Flagstaff
40
Big Sandy River
Winslow
Fort Mojave Reservation
Prescott National Forest
Verde River
Sedona
Coconino National Forest
191
Lake Havasu City
Prescott
Apache-Sitgreaves National Forest
Zuni Reservation
Lake Havasu
Alamo Lake
93
Santa Maria River
Tonto National Forest
Payson
Fort Apache Reservation
Bill Williams River
17
Eagar
Parker
Horseshoe Reservoir
60
Apache-Sitgreaves National Forest
Colorado River
Colorado River Tribes
60
Salt River Reservation
Bartlett Reservoir
Theodore Roosevelt Lake
Salt River
60
Tonto National Forest
San Carlos Apache Reservation
Black River
10
Glendale
Phoenix
Scottsdale
191
Gila River Reservation
Tempe
60
Globe
70
95
San Carlos Lake
Gila River
Ak-Chin Community
10
Florence
Gila River
8
Safford
Casa Grande
Yuma
8
Tenmile Wash
Brawley Wash
10
Coronado National Forest
San Simon River
191
Ajo
10
Organ Pipe Cactus National Monument
Tohono O'odham Nation
Tuscon
Coronado National Forest
San Xavier Reservation
191
N
W
E
S
19
Coronado National Forest
Bisbee
Coronado National Forest

Interstate Highways
U.S. Highways
City or Town
State Capital
Indian Reservation
National Monument
National Forest
National Park
National Recreation Area
Highest Point in the State
Only point in the U.S. common to four state corners

miles
0 20

Arizona March Song

Words by Margaret Rowe Clifford
Music by Maurice Blumenthal

f

Come __ to this land of sun - shine To this land where life is

young, Where the wide, wide world is wait - ing, The _ songs that will now be

sung. Where the gold - en sun is flam - ing In - to warm, white, shin - ing

day. And the sons of men are blaz - ing Their price - less right of

way. Sing the song that's in your hearts _ Sing _ of the great South -

west, Thank God for Ar - i - zon - a In splen - did sun - shine

dressed. For thy beau - ty and thy grand - eur, For thy re - gal robes so

sheen. We hail thee, Ar - i - zon - a, Our _ god-dess and our queen.

More About Arizona

Books

George, Jean Craighead. *One Day in the Desert.* New York: HarperCollins Children's Book Group, 1996.

Goff, John S. *Arizona, an Illustrated History of the Grand Canyon State.* Northridge, CA: Windsor Publications, 1988.

Magley, Beverly. *Arizona Wildflowers: a Children's Field Guide to the State's Most Common Wildflowers.* Helena, MT: Falcon Press, 1991.

Minor, Wendell. *Grand Canyon: Exploring a Natural Wonder.* New York: Blue Sky Press, 1998.

Moreillon, Judi. *Sing Down the Rain.* Santa Fe, NM: Kiva Publishing. 1997.

Roesel, Monty. *Songs from the Loom: A Navajo Girl Learns to Weave.* Minneapolis: Lerner Publications. 1995.

Web sites

Official State of Arizona Webpage:
http://www.az.gov/webapp/portal

Arizona Office of Tourism
http://www.arizonaguide.com

Sharlot Hall Museum
http://www.sharlot.org/index.shtml

About the Author

Kathleen Derzipilski is a research editor who specializes in children's nonfiction. She lives in San Diego, California.

Index

Page numbers in **boldface** are illustrations.

maps
  Arizona, **6, 76**
  United States, **1**

activity, 44-45, **44, 45**
African Americans, 42, 52-53, **52**
agriculture, 65-68, **66, 68**
Anasazi, 23-25, **24**
animals, 4-5, **4, 5,** 13, 13, 16-21, **17, 18, 19, 20, 21**
Apache,
  people, 25, 29, 30, **31,** 43, 46
  Wars, 29-30
Asian Americans, 42, 48-49, **49**

Basin and Range, 7, 12-13
birds, 4, **4**
Bisbee, 34
bola tie, 5, **5**
buttes, 8,

Canyon de Chelly, 25
Central Arizona Porject (CAP), 37-38, **38**
Chicanos. *See* Mexican American
civil rights, 52
Civil War, 29
cliff dwellings,
  See also Keet Seel Ruin
climate, 15-16
Cochise, 30
Colorado
  Plateau, 7-10,
  River, 8, **8,** 13, 29, 37-38

copper, 5, 34, 57, 68-69, 71, **71**
Coronado, Francisco Vásquez de, 26, **26**

dams, 13, 35, 69
desert, 12, 13, **13,**
  See also Sonora Desert
drought, 16, 25,

economy, 65-74
Europeans, 41-42,
exploration, 8, 26-30
  See also Coronado, Powell

farming, 25, 27, 33, **33,** 65-66, **65,** 68
festivals and events, 54-55, **54-55**
Flagstaff, 72
flowers, 4, **4**
Four Corners, 10

Gadsden Purchase, 29
Geronimo, 30, **31**
Goodwin, John, 29
government, 57-63
Grand Canyon, 8, **8**
grasslands, 33-34
Great Depression, 34

Hall, Sharlot, 51, **51**
history, 23-39
Hohokam, 25
Hopi, 24, 43
Hunt, George W.P., 50 , **50**

irrigation, 35, 37-38, **38,** 65

Kaibab
  National Forest, **22**
  Plateau, 9
Keet Seel Ruin, 24, **24**
Kitt Peak Observatory, 72, **72**

Latinos, 42, 46-47
livestock, 27, 33-34,
Lockwood, Lorna, 50, **50**
Long Walk, The, 30

manufacturing, 69
mesas, 8, 25
Mexican-American
  people, 46-47, **46**
  War, 28
Mexican Highland, 7, 11-12, **11**
Mingus, 51, **51**
mining, 5, 31-32, 33, 34, 68-69
missionaries, 26, 27
missions, 27, **27**
  See also San Xavier del Bac, Tumacácori
Mogollon, 25
Monument Valley, 10
mountains, 11,

national monuments, 24,
Native Americans, 5, **22,** 23-25, **24,** 28, 42-46, **43,** 57
  See also Anasazi, Apache, Hohokam, Hopi, Mogollon, Navajo, Pimas, Pueblo, Zuni
Navajo, **22,** 25, 29, 30, 42-45, **43**
Nogales, 28

O'odham, 26, 43

Painted Desert, 10, **11**
Phoenix, 11, **11,** 25, 41, 60
Pimas, 28
plants, 11, 13, **13,** 16-21, **18**
population, 41
Powell, John Wesley, 8, 39, **39**
Prescott, 29, 60
Pueblo, 23, 24

railroads, 29, 31, **31,** 32, **32,** 48
ranches and ranching, 33, **41,** 68, **68**
recipe, 67
rivers, 13-14

Salt River, 14, 25, 46
San Xavier del Bac, 27, **27**
settlers, 33
silver, 29, 31-21, 68-69
Sonora Desert, 12, 13, **13**
Spanish
  exploration, 26
  settlement, 27
state
  borders, 7
  capital, **56,** 60, **61**
  flag, 75, **75**
  name, 28
  nickname, 4
  seal, 75, **75**
  size, 7
  song, 77
  symbols, 4-5, **4-5**
statehood, 4, 34
Strug, Kerri, 50, **50**
Sunset Crater, 9, **9**
Sun City, 36-37, **36**

technology, 71, **71,** 72, **72**
Tempe, 41, 46
Territory of Arizona, 29
Tewanima, Lewis, 51, **51**
Theodore Roosevelt Dam, 14, 39, **39**
timeline, 39
Tombstone, 31
tourism, **64,** 65, 71, **71,** 73-74, **74**
Treaty of Guadalupe Hidalgo, 28
trees, 4, **4,** 11
Tubac, 28
Tucson, 12, 25, 29, 37, 41, **42,** 46, 60, 73
Tumacácori, 27
turquoise, 5, **5**

volcanoes, 9, **9**
voting, 59-60, **59,** 62-63

Web sites, 63, 78
wildlife, 16-21,
World War I, 34
World War II, 35, 48-49, 69

Yuma, 29

Zuni, 24